World Builder Mini

Essential World-Building for Fiction Writers

Connie Bauldree
Author by Design

World Builder Mini: Essential World-Building For Fiction Writers

Published by BaulConn Publishing www.authorbydesign.co www.writersblockboxes.com

First Edition: 2021

Introduction

This Mini gives you the essential framework for creating believable worlds that enhance your story without overwhelming it.

Focus on story-serving elements: Build only what affects your plot Start with basics, add details as needed Keep consistency over complexity Let your world enhance, not overshadow, your characters

How To Use This Mini:

1. Establish your World Foundation first
2. Map Physical Geography that matters to your story
3. Define Magic/Tech systems your characters encounter
4. Create relevant History that shapes your plot
5. Use Quick Reference sheets while writing

Remember: Great worlds feel lived-in. Include imperfections and mysteries. Not everything needs explanation. Focus on what serves your story.

World Foundation

Core Concept

What makes your world unique:

____

____

One-sentence world description:

____

____

Primary genre:

____

Time period/technology level:

____

____

World Identity

What inhabitants call their world:

____

What outsiders call it:

____

World's greatest strength:

____

World's greatest weakness:

____

Creation Basics

How was this world formed:

How long has it existed:

What inhabitants believe about origins:

What major changes shaped it:

Story Connection

How does your world create conflict:

What world rules will characters break:

What world secrets drive your plot:

Physical Geography Essentials

World Overview

World size and shape:

Land vs. water ratio:

Major continents or regions:

What separates these areas:

Important Locations

Most important location for your story:

Most dangerous area:

Hub of travel/trade:

Forbidden or mysterious place:

Climate & Environment

Major climate zones:

Seasonal patterns:

Natural disasters or dangers:

Environmental challenges:

Resources & Materials

Most vital resources:

Scarce or rare materials:

What resources cause conflicts:

How resources affect your plot:

Notes:

Magic Technology Systems

System Type

Circle what applies to your world:
High Magic / Low Magic / No Magic High Tech / Low Tech / Mixed Tech Magic + Technology / Magic vs. Technology

Basic Rules

How does magic/technology work:

Who can access it:

What are the limitations:

What does it cost to use:

System Impact

How does it affect daily life:

How does it change warfare:

How does it affect society:

What problems does it create:

Story Application
How do your characters use these systems:

What system rules will create conflict:

What happens when systems fail:

How will systems change during your story:

History & Background

Historical Eras

What are the major time periods:

Which era is considered the golden age:

What era was the darkest:

What era are you writing in:

Major Events

Most important historical event:

Greatest war or conflict:

Biggest disaster or catastrophe:

Most significant discovery:

Historical Figures

Most famous hero:

Most notorious villain:

Most influential leader:

Most mysterious figure:

Current Impact

How does history affect your story's present:

What historical conflicts still matter:

What historical secrets exist:

How do characters view their history:

Notes:

Creatures & Inhabitants

Dominant Species

What species rules or dominates:

How are they organized socially:

What are their strengths/weaknesses:

How do they view other species:

Other Intelligent Species

What other thinking beings exist:

How do different species interact:

What conflicts exist between species:

Which species are allies or enemies:

Animals & Creatures

Most common animals:

Most dangerous predators:

Animals used for work/transport:

Creatures that are magical or unusual:

Species Relationships

How do species cooperate:

What causes species conflicts:

How does species diversity affect your story:

What species changes will occur during your plot:

Notes:

Culture & Society Basics

Government Type

How is your world governed:

Who holds real power:

How are leaders chosen:

What laws are most important:

Social Structure

What are the social classes:

How do people gain status:

What creates social conflict:

How much social mobility exists:

Values & Beliefs

What does this culture value most:

What do they fear or hate:

What do they consider sacred:

What would shock them most:

Daily Life

What does a typical day look like:

How do people communicate:

What do people do for work:

How do people entertain themselves:

Notes:

Conflict & Tensions

External Threats

What outside forces threaten your world:

What other worlds or enemies exist:

What environmental dangers persist:

How do external threats unite or divide inhabitants:

Internal Conflicts

What groups fight within your world:

What resources are fought over:

What ideological conflicts exist:

____

____

What generational tensions persist:

____

____

Systemic Problems

What doesn't work well in your world:

____

____

What old systems are breaking down:

____

____

What new problems are emerging:

____

____

What changes are people resisting:

____

____

Story Conflicts

What world conflicts drive your plot:

How do world problems affect your characters:

What world tensions will escalate:

How will world conflicts resolve:

Notes:

World Integration Checklist

Consistency Check

- ☐ All world elements work together logically
- ☐ No major contradictions in world rules
- ☐ Magic/tech systems have clear limitations
- ☐ History explains current world state
- ☐ Geography affects culture and politics

Story Service Check

- ☐ World elements create obstacles for characters
- ☐ World conflicts drive plot forward
- ☐ World rules create story tension
- ☐ World details enhance rather than distract
- ☐ World changes support character growth

Reader Experience Check

- ☐ World feels lived-in and real
- ☐ World details are revealed naturally
- ☐ World complexity matches story needs
- ☐ World surprises feel logical in hindsight
- ☐ World enhances emotional impact

Quick Reference Notes

Key world rules to remember:

Important world details for this story:

World elements that will surprise readers:

World changes that will occur during story:

World Summary Template

Essential World Info

World name:

Genre/time period:

Technology level:

Magic level:

Dominant species:

Key Locations

Primary setting:

Secondary locations:

Dangerous areas:

Important travel routes:

Hidden or secret places:

Power Structures

Government type:

Real power holders:

Major conflicts:

External threats:

Internal tensions:

Story Elements

World conflicts affecting plot:

World rules characters will break:

World secrets to be revealed:

World changes during story:

How world serves your specific story:

Notes Section

Additional world details:

Questions to explore later:

World elements still in development:

Notes:

About The Author

Connie Bauldree is a self-published author with a passion for storytelling and helping others craft their own. Writing under the pen names Connie Connolly, Emersyn Kane, Payton Rome, and Connie Bauldree, she has authored over 40 non-fiction writing resources and published nine fiction novels spanning multiple genres.

Connie is the owner of Author by Design, the creative hub behind the Builder Series and the Writer's Block Box, resources designed to inspire and empower writers at every stage of their journey. She is also the co-founder of SisterScribe Academy, a platform dedicated to supporting and educating aspiring authors.

Connie believes every writer has a story worth telling and is passionate about providing the tools and frameworks to help them succeed.

When she's not writing or developing innovative tools for authors, Connie enjoys connecting with her audience on social media. Follow her @authorbydesign for tips, updates, and inspiration.

Stay in touch and explore her offerings by signing up for her newsletter at www.authorbydesign.co. or www.writersblockboxes.com.